"Everything was
different
BEFORE IT CHANGED."

— *On a Versace shirt in a Dallas store window*

— *?* —

What should you do
when you're not sure what
you should be doing?

Sooner or later, we all face this kind of situation.
So what's your first impulse?

When uncertainty clouds the future, people generally
set about trying to eliminate it. There's nothing wrong
with wanting to minimize our "not knowing," but here's
the dilemma: Sometimes uncertainty won't yield to our
efforts . . . we personally can't make it go away. Even if our
natural inclination is to get rid of the uncertainty, often
we just have to *be* with it.

This doesn't mean you should resort to a wait-and-see
attitude. You can wait-and-do, busying yourself in productive,
gratifying, peace-giving ways while uncertainty has its
hour. You can use this vague, ambiguous time for your own
discovery and growth . . . for uncommon accomplish-
ments.

The key is to manage yourself instead of trying to manage the
uncertainty. But don't count on your instincts to guide you —
doing what comes naturally leads to self-defeating behavior.
Uncertainty requires special treatment, counter-intuitive
moves, before it will reveal to you its best possibilities.

Is it worth the effort? The rewards go far beyond what
you might imagine.

This time and circumstance, whether troubling or
promising, may not be of your own choosing. But this is
your life unfolding — *your creation* — and you will own
what emerges from this uncertainty.

Create wisely.

PRITCHETT

The Unfolding

— *chapter 1* —

Embrace
uncertainty.

WHAT IF YOU COULD ELIMINATE UNCERTAINTY? Would you actually have the guts to do that? Do you have the strange notion that you'd be happier, more successful, or otherwise better off in a world that you could totally, accurately predict?

Keep in mind, now, that life wouldn't change per se. Your five senses would still work the same way. You'd still face success and failure, so-called good days and bad. You'd be the very same person, in the same old world, married to your same existence — for better or for worse, for richer or for poorer, in sickness and in health — till death you did part. (Oh, by the way, you'd see *that* coming, too.)

Nothing else different than before. Just no surprises. No unknowns. No guesswork.

But, of course, the elimination of uncertainty would change everything. *Profoundly.* And you would suffer unbearable feelings of loss. The tension on this string of everyday living — something we take so for granted, and so often complain about — would go slack. The sparkle of anticipation would vanish, the delight in things unexpected would disappear. Hope, all of a sudden, would become a meaningless concept. Your positive emotions would flat-line. Life would become bleak. Desolate.

This uncertainty that we too easily curse would soon be seen in a totally different light. We would quickly discover that it's a precious condition, a catalyst for meaning in life, a force for shaping our individual destinies. Given a second chance, we would rush to embrace uncertainty. Passionately. We'd seize the opportunity to experience fully this vague and uncharted space, grateful for the chance to define ourselves better by how we choose to live our way through the fog. We would devour these limbo days, hungry to see how they evolve, savoring the raw "becoming" that is the essence of being alive.

The Unfolding

Uncertainty offers us an opening into a future we can help design today, even as it further influences who we shall be tomorrow. Sure, much about the situation lies beyond our control. And uncertainty may carry with it some bad outcomes. But then life always leaves scars, just as surely as it eventually leaves us altogether.

The wisdom lies in our approaching uncertain times not just as a problem, not merely as a threatening lull where we wait helplessly for our fate to arrive. Instead, we should look at it as a grace period, a staging interval where more of our life is being born. Viewed from that angle, we could consider it a gift, one whose treasure will be defined by how we choose to participate in this unfolding of our world and our selves.

"A person who claims personal authority is no longer a victim."

— Angeles Arrien, *The Four-Fold Way*

chapter 2

Do a double-take on the hand you've been dealt.

HERE YOU ARE, STARING AT THE CARDS LIFE HAS HANDED YOU. And looking back is a "full house" of questions . . . a fistful of uncertainty.

At first glance maybe you figure this situation doesn't offer you a half decent chance of winning. But life refuses to shuffle and re-deal. Nobody gets to discard and draw again. Finally, you're not even allowed to fold — one way or another, this is your hand to play.

Ok. So long as you're here at the table, let's study the cards a little more carefully.

It helps to know a few things about human nature. Let's start with the fact that people have a highly predictable reaction to uncertainty: *Our first scan is for danger.* It's a behavior pattern rooted deep in our survival instincts. We're just wired that way as human beings. As playwright John Dryden put it, "Self-defense is Nature's oldest law." And that's what gets triggered when life stacks the deck with uncertainty.

What complicates things is that some people seem unable to get past this first reaction. Their first take is their only take — all they can see in the cards are bad things to come. Naturally, this mindset by itself can knock them out of the game. Nobody's going to perform well if they think only in terms of losing. To bring out our best, and to lift the odds that things actually unfold in our favor, we must consider the potential upside.

So back to the cards for a second look.

This time, disregard the danger signs. The double-take is for refocusing. Move beyond the natural reflex that prompted you to see uncertainty from a negative slant. Think further, out past your first primal imaginings, where that instinctive wariness yields to a more open-minded view of the situation. Use this second scan to search for more promising possibilities, for openings where you can help influence good outcomes.

The Unfolding

Now frankly, your present frame of mind may be such that you actually resent this idea of a positive double-take. And sometimes it proves almost impossible to pull off — especially when you feel angry, heartsick, afraid . . . even desperate. Danger, or the sense of loss, has a very strong magnetic pull on our attention and concentration. As the saying goes, "Bad news chases good news away." The dark clouds capture our attention well before we're inclined to go looking for silver linings. Uncertainty typically makes its threats prior to revealing its opportunities.

Just lean back for a bit. Study the situation. It might turn out that you're sitting there holding one helluva hand. And it could be that it all comes down to how you play those cards.

Life often turns on such little things.

"If we recognize that change and uncertainty are basic principles, we can greet the future and the transformation we are undergoing with the understanding that we do not know enough to be pessimistic."

— Hazel Henderson,
The Politics of the Solar Age

— *chapter 3* —

Think in
the direction
of strength.

THE MIND DECIDES WHAT
TO MAKE OF A SITUATION.

Like whether it's good or
bad . . . what it means . . .
how we should feel.

Thoughts create our "reality" and shape our response. While the mind
tries to nail it correctly, sometimes the brain does things that deceive
us. Sizing up our world in a haze of uncertainty — as "through a glass
darkly" — the mind conspires with our primitive instincts, predisposing
us to think in negative directions.

We justify this outlook on the grounds that we're "being careful." Our
worries and concerns make sense to us. We rely on them to somehow
provide us an element of protection, as if dwelling on threats to our
well-being reduces our vulnerability.

But what if the exact opposite is happening?

Psychological research proves that negative thinking weakens us in many ways. In fact, after warning us to "be careful," pessimistic thoughts and emotions offer no further benefits whatsoever, contributing instead to a broad range of problems. We become less resilient. Our creativity and problem-solving abilities deteriorate. We lose confidence, and have more difficulty adapting to change. Negativity even weakens our immune systems.

You might be surprised, but this isn't a pitch for positive thinking. It's to emphasize the importance of *non-negative* thinking.

If this sounds confusing, it's probably because you're used to the old idea that optimism and pessimism represent opposite ends of the same scale. But new research indicates that they're actually two different scales. Further, these studies reveal that it's not more positive thinking that benefits us most, but *less negative thinking*. To put it another way, optimism isn't as good as pessimism is bad.

A negative outlook takes us toward weakness. Toward problems and unhappiness. Toward all that might go wrong as the situation unfolds.

The Unfolding

The result? We feel diminished, even more vulnerable, maybe helpless —
all this at the very time we need access to our best inner resources. So-called
carefulness that's anchored in negativity fails to protect us. We're safer
approaching uncertainty more *carelessly.*

When the "givens" we took for granted are coming undone, we're facing a
future of fresh possibilities. We've come upon an important crossroad in
life. Better for us to loosen up rather than tighten up . . . relax instead of
resisting . . . open ourselves to possibilities instead of obsessing about
problems. We should think, and live, in the direction of our strengths.

It's time to pause, asking, "What is trying to happen here . . . in this
situation . . . in me and my world? How shall I release myself to participate in this unfolding?"

"Deep down we know that to cooperate with fate brings great personal power and responsibility."

— Joseph Jaworski, *Synchronicity*

chapter 4

Commit yourself to full use of the present.

WE GO ALONG IN LIFE BEHAVING THE WAY WE DO BECAUSE EACH OF US HAS OUR OWN PARTICULAR VIEW OF THE FUTURE.

Our ordinary intent is to use *now* in ways that position us acceptably for the *later* we expect.

That works fairly well until uncertainty hits. Then our sense of predictability fades. It's harder to "expect" accurately. The new unknowns break our patterns of everyday living, forcing us to rethink what we should do with ourselves. But we're dealing with a fuzzier future. There's more guesswork in trying to figure out what *later* is going to look like. This causes some people to quit using their *now* effectively.

In *Deep Survival*, author Laurence Gonzales writes, "Freezing is a classic emotional response of all mammals." And you'll see this in people who are confronted by a wide range of crises or stressful situations, including uncertainty. There's a tendency to freeze up, paralyzed by the surprise, the ambiguity, the lack of predictability.

But if uncertainty could talk, it would say, "Don't use me as an excuse to go into a holding pattern. And don't presume helplessness. *Control the controllables.*" We'd be instructed to commit ourselves fully to constructive use of the present — not a gritty, trying harder, will power attempt to eliminate uncertainty, but a commitment to engage fully in the unfolding of things.

There are important moves you're free to make in spite of the uncertainty . . . or maybe because of it. If this feels like a waiting game, the question is, "How productively will you choose to wait?"

Maybe you feel trapped in time, a victim of circumstances, like Bill Murray in the movie classic, *Groundhog Day*. So how long will you resist and fight against the situation — can you get past resentment, anger, or blame? Will you give up in the face of so many unknowns? Do you choose to waste the present merely because the future seems unclear?

The Unfolding

You could, of course, decide to use these days to their full capacity. You could pack uncertainty's hollowness with rich new meaning of your own design.

Sometimes people who feel lost in uncertainty end up finding themselves for the first time in their lives. They discover precious things, in both themselves and their world, that otherwise never would have been found.

Unfolding has, as one of its meanings, "to develop fully." Let today's uncertainty carry you in that direction.

"Waiting, done at really high speeds, will frequently look like something else."

— Carrie Fisher

chapter 5

Use intention to shape your future.

Uncertainty limits our visibility into what lies ahead.

But we shouldn't presume that it forces the same limitations on our personal intentions.

Too often our reasoning goes something like this: "Ummm, I can't tell how this is going to turn out. There are so many unknowns. I'd better pull back, let things sort themselves out, before I set my mind on what I want to happen." On the surface, this sort of thinking makes sense. But the logic is flawed, because it means forfeiting a power we have within ourselves to shape outcomes. It's a mindset that invites even more drift into our lives.

This uncertainty — the situation you now face — is not something happening *to* you. It is happening *with* you. You have an active role in how this episode spools out over the days to come. You're not separate from it. The new shape of things will materialize in flowing through you, and one of the best ways to influence how life unfolds for you personally is through your intentions.

So set your intent. Focus on the particular outcome you seek. Be very clear in your mind about what you want or need. But make it effortless — gentle resolve, not intense willing.

Proceeding with deliberate intent for a particular end result changes the dynamics of the situation. You introduce a new force, one that functions on your behalf to bring forth what you want or need.

Exactly how does this work?

First let's explore the physiological basis for the power of intention. At the base of your brain lies a little bundle of cells called the reticular activating system, or RAS. It sifts, sorts, and evaluates incoming signals — everything you see, hear, touch, smell, or taste — deciding what deserves your attention and what can more or less be ignored. The RAS filters your full range of experiences. Usually only three things are allowed access to your consciousness: things that you value, things that are unique or unusual, and things that threaten you. Intention activates this attention center in your brain, positioning it to serve you as an incredible source of power and creativity. Clear, purposeful intent tells the RAS how to adjust its filters. Then it goes hunting, sifting through your entire range of experiences for things that relate to the fulfillment of your intention.

For a second and more exotic explanation for the power of intention, we can turn to quantum physics. This cutting edge science suggests that intention connects us to a Universal Source, an infinite energy field, that enables us in our pursuits. Maybe this seems too far-out for you. But today's most respected physicists point to research that supports this position.

So whether you consider how the brain works, or how our universe functions, you need to treat intention as an active force. It's a mental agent that can help us create the world we want. And we should use it to aim our way through uncertainty.

BOOKS BY PRITCHETT, LP

pritchettnet.com

TIGHTLY WRITTEN AND IMPACTFUL, OUR HANDBOOKS GIVE FRESH, HONEST, AND POINTED MESSAGES ABOUT CHANGE FROM EXPERT AUTHORS.
PRITCHETT OFFERS TOTAL INTEGRATED SOLUTIONS: TRAINING, KEYNOTES, CONSULTING, AND COACHING PROGRAMS WHICH CAN BE CUSTOMIZED FOR YOUR SPECIFIC SITUATION.

Change

PRITCHETT's *Complete Set*

Obtain the entire collection of PRITCHETT's handbooks. Refer to this library over and over as your company encounters new change situations—merger/acquisition, reorganization, culture change, etc.

Deep Strengths: Getting to the Heart of High Performance (Hardback)

A new, breakthrough model for "strength training" that will enhance leadership effectiveness, improve employee performance, plus build a culture best suited for today's knowledge workers and the relentless pace of change.

training

consulting

Business As UnUsual: The Handbook for Managing and Supervising Organizational Change

A "quick impact" manual with 27 guidelines for successfully managing organizational change. Discover how to become a change agent, protect profits, build corporate momentum, and improve productivity during transition and change. **Over 1,000,000 copies sold!**

training

The Employee Handbook for Organizational Change

Teaches employees the differences between myth and reality during times of rapid change. Provides practical tips to help employees take personal control and face problems with a constructive attitude. **Over 1,000,000 copies sold!**

training

The Employee Handbook of New Work Habits for a Radically Changing World

Uses hard facts and powerful logic to corner the reader with the reality of how he or she must change because of the radical shifts in the world. Provides 13 clear and practical guidelines workers can immediately weave into their daily routines. **Over 2,000,000 copies sold!**

training

The Employee Handbook of New Work Habits for The Next Millenium: 10 New Ground Rules for Job Success

The sequel to the best-selling *New Work Habits for a Radically Changing World*. Provides your employees with 10 guidelines for improving performance—without sacrificing control of their personal lives in the process.

Firing Up Commitment During Organizational Change: A Handbook for Managers

Equips your management team with 14 tightly-focused guidelines for building job commitment in the face of fast-paced change.

training

BOOKS BY PRITCHETT, LP

pritchettnet.com

Change

Resistance: Moving Beyond the Barriers to Change

Contains 16 guidelines for countering the single biggest barrier to beneficial change—*employee resistance*. This handbook shows your staff how to re-channel precious energy, get aligned, and focus on moving your organization forward.

training

Service Excellence!

Delivers a powerful 2-step strategy for winning and keeping customers in today's demanding marketplace. A robust but elegantly simple approach that makes the job easier yet more effective.

training

A Survival Guide to the Stress of Organizational Change

Shows employees how they can avoid 15 basic mistakes that create major stress in the workplace. It explains the sources and provides practical, usable tips for reducing stress. **Over 1,000,000 copies sold!**

training

Team ReConstruction: Building A High Performance Work Group During Change

Provides a 14-point strategy for building and leading teams in the wake of explosive organizational change. Instructs on making quick repairs and mobilizing employees to shorten transitions and protect operating efficiency.

training

Teamwork: The Team Member Handbook

Provides 16 guidelines for turning any group into a tightly-knit, high-powered team capable of achieving outstanding results.

training

The Unfolding: A Handbook for Living Strong, Being Effective, and Knowing Happiness During Uncertain Times

Change and uncertainty go hand in hand…but uncertainty often causes most of the problems. These 9 powerful "counter-intuitive moves" reduce people's feelings of helplessness, protect productivity, and set the stage for successful organizational change.

training

Mergers

After the Merger: The Authoritative Guide for Integration Success (Hardback)

Provides a clear look at the tasks and problems of post-merger management. It offers straightforward recommendations on dealing with employee bailouts, productivity and morale problems, power struggles, employees being recruited away from the firm, staffing duplication, and much more. **Named one of the top ten business books of the year by *Library Journal*.**

training

consulting

The Employee Guide to Mergers and Acquisitions

The all-time best-selling book on mergers. Answers employees' hot questions about what happens during a merger. Gives them 10 easy-to-follow "survival steps." **Over 1,000,000 copies sold!**

training

consulting

Mergers

training

consulting

Making Mergers Work: A Guide to Managing Mergers and Acquisitions

Offers specific suggestions on how to avoid the high cost of merger failure, improve productivity, protect market share, and overcome resistance to change. A very practical guidebook for managing the merger integration process.

training

consulting

Mergers: Growth in the Fast Lane

Presents 10 guidelines on how to win in the new merger game—how to deal with differences in corporate culture, handle resistance, and manage merger-specific communications; also lists the dangers of being politically correct in management.

training

consulting

Smart Moves: A Crash Course on Merger Integration Management

This is the voice of merger experience put into print. Presents 16 essential guidelines designed to dramatically improve your odds for success.

Culture

training

consulting

Culture Shift: The Employee Handbook for Changing Corporate Culture

Provides an entirely new mindset for your staff, quickly transforming behavior throughout the entire organization to create a more flexible, adaptable culture. The 16 compelling guidelines offer a clear blueprint for creating a culture that thrives on change.

training

consulting

The Employee Handbook for Shaping Corporate Culture: The Mission Critical Approach to Culture Integration and Culture Change

Delivers a crucial all-employee message on the "how-to's" of culture integration and change. This handbook will help your entire workforce focus on the *mission critical* 5%.

training

consulting

High-Velocity Culture Change: A Handbook for Managers

A direct, usable, real-world message on how to change corporate culture, with 22 specific guidelines for high-velocity transformation.

Process Improvement

training

consulting

Improving Performance: How to Manage the White Space on the Organization Chart (Hardback)

With over 100,000 copies sold worldwide, this is recognized as the book that launched the process improvement revolution. This book is "the process bible" for anyone interested in performance improvement consulting.

training

consulting

Managing Sideways: Using the Rummler-Brache Process Improvement Approach to Achieve Performance Breakthrough

Gives the most important ground rules and critical success factors for becoming a process-centric, performance-driven organization.

The Breakthrough Principle of 16x: Real Simple Innovation for 16 Times Better Results

Richard Koch, author of *The 80/20 Principle*, offers a realistic ready-to-use innovation process for doing things differently, with no more energy, to get 16 times better results.

training

The Ethics of Excellence

The 18 powerful guidelines in this book will teach your team to protect integrity and public image, build pride and loyalty, plus improve product and service quality at the same time.

Fast Growth: A Career Acceleration Strategy

Emphasizes the importance of a willingness to "align—adapt—add value." Teaches employees how to protect their career by contributing value to the organization.

Hard Optimism: How to Succeed in a World Where Positive Wins (Hardback)

Helps your people develop the thought patterns that build resilience…that serve as a buffer against stress…that energize, empower, and enhance performance in virtually all circumstances.

training

The Leadership Engine: Building Leaders at Every Level

This handbook is a quick-read version of the best seller by Noel Tichy and Eli Cohen, *The Leadership Engine: How Winning Companies Build Leaders at Every Level*.

training

Topgrading: How to Hire, Coach and Keep A Players

The platinum standard for hiring, coaching, and keeping top talent. This handbook is based on the bestselling hardcover book, *Topgrading*, by Bradford D. Smart, Ph.D.

training

The Quantum Leap Strategy

A sequel to *you²*, the book that originally outlined the unique formula for achieving quantum leaps in performance. You and your team will learn how to capture the magic of paradigm shifts, tap tremendous hidden potential, and tackle tough organizational problems.

you²: A High-Velocity Formula for Multiplying Your Personal Effectiveness in Quantum Leaps

Promotes an unconventional strategy for achieving breakthrough performance. This powerful approach replaces the concept of attaining gradual, incremental success through massive effort.

ORDER ONLINE AT www.pritchettnet.com

OR CALL 800.992.5922

"Thought creates the world
and then says 'I didn't do it.'"

— David Bohm, physicist
(Quoted by Peter Senge in *Synchronicity*)

chapter 6

Let nothing break your spirit.

UNCERTAINTY IS AN ENEMY OF THE HEART. It preys on the human spirit. We need to remember this, and defend ourselves against its demoralizing influence on our emotional wellbeing.

Our spirit is one of the most precious things in life. Though invisible — like gravity, wind, or magnetism — it's a powerful force that permeates our personal world. In fact, it lays the foundation for our life experience. Spirit is far more than mere "attitude." It's a mysterious blend of emotional strength, energy, mental outlook, character, passion, and will. You might think of it as the X-factor in life, the internal force that can defy circumstances, helping us rise to whatever occasion we face.

You know what it feels like when your spirit is strong. You feel enabled. You're sturdy and buoyant. Spirit juices you up for the challenges of life — it helps you believe in yourself, gives you resilience, and brings out your best. Other people — even animals — warm to it. Spirit is the antidote of choice for the discomforts of uncertainty.

Sometimes a highly charged spirit just comes naturally. But at those times when it fails us — when we allow this inner fire to flicker and fade — then uncertainty steals its way into the heart. A weak spirit lets worry take hold. We begin to doubt ourselves . . . question the possibilities . . . maybe feel like a victim. This is when we have to claw our way out of deep, dark cisterns of fear, loss, or pure undiluted defeat.

So how can we do this? Better still, what might we do to protect and even strengthen the spirit?

Well, it can be as simple as vowing to ourselves that we absolutely refuse to surrender our spirit to circumstances. We can reach deep within, to the far corners of our psyche, tapping the quiet emotional reserves that ordinarily go untouched. We can pull forth the makings of an iron will that refuses to bow to troubling or painful times.

The Unfolding

People do this every day, amazing themselves at their fortitude, their emotional fiber, their raw inner strength. These are our heroic acts, the shining moments that reveal our best character even as they further build it. Spirit is emotional muscle, and it responds to exercise. When it's tested is when it gets a chance to grow. You can build your spirit by facing reality straight on — accepting what is — and resolving to be big enough to take it, however much it hurts.

This is not meant to deny grief . . . let it have its proper moment. If grief can bring healing value, give those feelings time to do their work. But grief should be a passing thing, a transient, not a long term resident aching inside your chest and draining the life force from you. Your ability to restore yourself emotionally will determine how your future unfolds.

Here lies the secret to mastering the psychology of uncertainty:
Never underestimate the power of the human spirit.

"It is only when the moment of crisis comes that we discover whether we actually have the power of the heart."

— Lewis B. Smedes, *A Pretty Good Person*

chapter 7

Live with
the long view.

THE MOST IMPORTANT TIME TO OPERATE WITH
THE LONG VIEW IS WHEN THE FUTURE SEEMS
MOST UNCERTAIN.

Problem is, uncertainty pulls our attention toward the situation that's close at hand. We become preoccupied with what's going on short-range. Then what happens? We behave as if present circumstances will dictate how our future develops. Instead, we should rely on our long view of the future to guide how we deal with our present circumstances.

You have a life story unfolding here, and you're the primary author as well as the main character. How do you want this story to turn out?

The author E. L. Doctorow said, "Writing a novel is like driving at night in the fog. You can only see as far as your headlights, but you can make the whole trip that way." The important thing is to write through the uncertainty — to write with the *story* in mind — even though it's hard to predict what's coming next or know for sure how the story will end.

So think strategically. Keep moving forward, creatively and purposefully, with the book of your life in mind. Let your day-to-day tactics be shaped by your long view.

A far-reaching perspective gives you a more balanced view of the present. Here's a case in point. Research shows that human beings have a far greater sensitivity to losses than to gains. In fact, losses can carry twice the psychological impact of gains. So when we assess the potential risks associated with uncertainty, our short-term gamble will normally be warped. We'll much prefer to take risks that might avoid a possible loss than take risks to achieve a possible gain. To put it another way, we're far more concerned about what uncertainty might take from us than what good it might bring. We should adjust our lens to give us a view with more depth of field.

The Unfolding

Now, you may want to consider several different scenarios as possible roads you might have to travel in writing your story. Scenario planning is a process for rehearsing the future. The idea is to imagine alternatives to what seems like the most probable or "official" future if current trend lines are projected forward. And why go through this mental exercise? Because creating an array of plausible yet quite different scenarios will challenge your assumptions. Preparing for multiple futures stretches your thinking in new directions. It prepares you for potential surprises and adds flexibility in support of your long view.

Much of what life brings our way, of course, lies beyond our control — we're only in charge of how we prepare and react. We each must craft our personal story around the future we anticipate and, then, around the realities we actually encounter. Still, we can prepare and react in keeping with the big story we carry inside.

The plot will sometimes shift on us unexpectedly. The periods of uncertainty can be disorienting. But the inner compass that will help us keep our bearings is the long view.

"Most people think of the future as
the ends and the present as the means,
whereas, in fact, the present is the ends
and the future is the means."

— Fritz Roethlisberger
(Quoted by Pascale, Milleman, and
Gioja in *Surfing the Edge of Chaos*)

— *chapter 8* —

Let go of what's going away.

MY SISTER, POLLY LOUISE, IS FIGHTING CANCER . . . maybe being reborn by the disease. Right now I couldn't tell you how it will turn out. But what I so admire is how she isn't giving up. She's just giving.

I watch from a distance, admiring her attention to things other than herself. I see her generosity, the desire to be productive, a conscientious attention to others and to her everyday duties. And I am amazed. What impresses me most is my sister's acceptance of what *is* . . . the absence of any complaining or bitterness about her condition . . . the stunning degree of gratitude for what remains rather than any lament whatsoever for what may have been lost.

This is real living. It's raw. Scary. She's sick to her very core, with deadening fatigue. Yet it seems she's discovered within herself a peculiar new strength in her capacity to carry on through this uncertainty. It hits me as noble behavior — character tested and found true — the wisdom to open herself to what good the unfolding might bring rather than hanging on in futile desperation to what is moving into her past.

There seems to be a piercingly clear logic at work in her heart and mind, a realization that the acceptance of what *is* represents the only solid foundation upon which to build our tomorrows. That, together with hope.

We free ourselves for the future by surrendering — by letting go of what's going away — and by allying ourselves with the state of affairs that we find unfolding before us. This acceptance liberates and empowers us. It clears the mind and conserves our emotional energy for constructive effort. Letting go, allowing ourselves to live straight into the uncertainty, opens us to new possibilities. We're free to *become.* In turning loose of what's obviously leaving, we cross the threshold for personal growth and discovery. And we have our fullest selves available to address whatever challenges or opportunities lie ahead.

The Unfolding

This is the heroic approach for dealing with uncertainty. And it's a personal choice.

Life doesn't force upon us any particular reaction — we each decide how we'll handle the slings and arrows that we're unable to dodge. Some people indulge in suffering, opting for the role of victim and seeking pity for themselves or guilt on the part of others. Some invest themselves in anger and blame — another victim approach — which more or less presumes that the solution to their predicament resides with those who "caused" the situation to happen. Both of these strategies represent a failure to let go. And both are prisons, making us captives of pain and unhappiness, withholding from us the promise of our best possible future.

Our destiny lies ahead — not with things that are going away, but that are yet to come — and this is where we should invest ourselves.

"Let it be; it will anyway."

— Unknown

chapter 9

Reserve judgment on the present until it becomes the past.

Tomorrows often look very different when they become our yesterdays.

Maybe the situation you're experiencing now feels undesirable and difficult. And maybe you expect it to damage your future. But one of these days you're likely to see all this in a very different light.

Human beings actually aren't very good at forecasting how they'll feel about things later on. As Harvard psychologist Daniel Gilbert puts it in his book, *Stumbling on Happiness,* "Our imagination has a hard time telling us how we will *think* about the future when we get there." And why do we predict so poorly? It's because our predictions about how we'll feel in the future are heavily influenced by our current emotions and state of mind. So if you're feeling bad about what's happening now, that will give you a negative bias about things to come.

It's just our nature to try to do things or create conditions that we're convinced can make us happy. Likewise, we try hard to avoid situations which we believe would be painful or difficult to endure. Meanwhile, research proves over and over that people mispredict how they'll eventually feel. Good things commonly fail to gratify as we expected, and misfortune often ends up being deemed a blessing in disguise. Dr. Gilbert adds, "We seem to know so little about the hearts and minds of the people we're about to become. Our ability to imagine our future emotions is flawed."

The lesson here is that so much of our current worry will surely turn out to be wasted effort. We have a marvelous ability to adapt, but a surprising inability to foresee what will prove to be the richest, most fulfilling aspects of our lives. Might today's challenges merely be the rites of passage to something better still?

The most important aspect of any situation is how you react to it. In fact, a person might react poorly to good things, or constructively to bad things, actually reversing the nature of circumstances. Such is the power we have within.

The Unfolding

You see proof of this all the time. Faced with the very same turn of events — whether good, bad, or uncertain — some people shape the situation to their benefit, while others end up disadvantaged. Dealing with identical circumstances, they produce completely different outcomes. This is not to say that we can always make things turn out the way we want. But we can devote ourselves, totally, to making the best of whatever comes our way. That commitment positions us to wield the most positive influence over how our lives unfold.

Often the potential good that's incubating during difficult or uncertain periods will reveal itself only with the passing of time. Our charge for now is to have faith in this latent promise, and do our personal best to bring it forth.

"I'm glad I'm not as unhappy
as I once thought I was."

— Scott Levesque, of the band *Wheat*

The Endnote

"We often see only what we are looking for and are readily distracted from observing what should be fairly obvious.

If we keep our focus narrow, we will probably not notice the big picture.

But in a world of unexpected and radical changes, we will need to widen our lenses in order to make sense of our unfolding, and often surprising, reality."

— Eamonn Kelly, *Powerful Times: Rising to the Challenge of Our Uncertain World*

Books by PRITCHETT, LP

Change Management

- *The 4th Level of Change*
- *Business As UnUsual: The Handbook for Managing and Supervising Organizational Change*
- *The Employee Handbook for Organizational Change*
- *The Employee Handbook of New Work Habits for a Radically Changing World: 13 Ground Rules for Job Success*
- *Firing Up Commitment During Organizational Change*
- *Hard Optimism: How to Succeed in a World Where Positive Wins*
- *MindShift: The Employee Handbook for Understanding the Changing World of Work*
- *Resistance: Moving Beyond the Barriers to Change*
- *A Survival Guide to the Stress of Organizational Change*
- *The Unfolding: A Handbook for Living Strong, Being Effective, and Knowing Happiness During Uncertain Times*

Growth & Innovation

- *The Breakthrough Principle of 16x: Real Simple Innovation for 16 Times Better Results*
- *Fast Growth: A Career Acceleration Strategy*
- *The Mars Pathfinder Approach to "Faster-Better-Cheaper"*
- *The Quantum Leap Strategy*
- *you^2: A High-Velocity Formula for Multiplying Your Personal Effectiveness in Quantum Leaps*

Corporate Culture

- *Culture Shift: The Employee Handbook for Changing Corporate Culture*
- *The Employee Handbook for Shaping Corporate Culture: The Mission Critical Approach to Culture Integration and Culture Change*
- *High-Velocity Culture Change: A Handbook for Managers*

Leadership & Teamwork

- *Carpe Mañana: 10 Critical Leadership Practices for Managing Toward the Future*

- *Deep Strengths: Getting to the Heart of High Performance*

- *The Leadership Engine Handbook: Building Leaders at Every Level*

- *Team ReConstruction: Building a High Performance Work Group During Change*

- *Teamwork: The Team Member Handbook*

Mergers & Acquisitions

- *After the Merger: The Authoritative Guide for Integration Success*

- *The Employee Guide to Mergers and Acquisitions*

- *Making Mergers Work: A Guide to Managing Mergers and Acquisitions*

- *Mergers: Growth in the Fast Lane*

- *Smart Moves: A Crash Course on Merger Integration Management*

Other

- *The Ethics of Excellence*

- *Improving Performance: How to Manage the White Space on the Organizational Chart*

- *Managing Sideways: Using the Rummler-Brache Process Improvement Approach to Achieve Breakthrough Performance*

- *Outsourced: 12 New Rules for Running Your Career in an Interconnected World*

- *Service Excellence!*

- *Solution #1: The Handbook for Workplace Fitness and Health*

- *Topgrading: How to Hire, Coach and Keep A Players*

For information regarding PRITCHETT's training, keynotes, and consulting built around our handbooks, please call **800-992-5922**.

About the Author

Price Pritchett is Chairman and CEO of
PRITCHETT, LP, a Dallas-based consulting
and training firm with offices in eight
other countries. He holds a Ph.D. in
psychology and has spent 30 years advising
top management in major corporations,
governmental organizations, and not-for-
profits. His work has taken him to Europe,
Asia, and throughout the Americas.

Dr. Pritchett's specialized work in merger
integration, organizational change, and corporate culture has been
referenced in most of the major business journals and newspapers. He
also has been featured on CNN, CNBC, and other major television networks.
With over 20 million copies of his books in print worldwide, he is one of
the best-selling business authors in the world. Virtually all of the *Fortune*
500 companies have used some combination of PRITCHETT's consulting,
training, and publications.

In *The Unfolding* he combines his deep background of experience with the
findings of disciplined science, providing research-proven techniques for lift-
ing the effectiveness of individuals and organizations.

Turning
Uncertainty Into Opportunity

Why is uncertainty so stressful and damaging to productivity?

It triggers feelings of helplessness. People lose focus and default to a wait-and-see stance that stalls progress. Negative attitudes and behavior patterns dull the edge of performance. Managers flounder because they're unskilled at dealing with the complex dynamics of uncertainty.

How can you protect operating effectiveness during times like these?

Our ½-day workshop—*Turning Uncertainty Into Opportunity*—positions your people to manage today's turmoil and adjust to the vague, uncertain future that confronts us. The session—

- Coaches on how to "wait-and-do" versus "wait-and-see"
- Teaches people how to avoid feeling like a victim
- Distinguishes productive from non-productive worry
- Identifies counter-intuitive moves for navigating through uncertainty
- Highlights typical reactions that sabotage people and teaches them ways to tap into their hidden resources
- Shifts attitudes and shapes behavior for successful transition & change

Call 800-992-5922 or visit us at
www.pritchettnet.com
for more information about delivery options and scheduling.

The
Unfolding

1-49 copies	____ copies at $7.95 each
50-99 copies	____ copies at $7.50 each
100-999 copies	____ copies at $6.95 each
1,000-4,999 copies	____ copies at $6.75 each
5,000-9,999 copies	____ copies at $6.50 each
10,000 or more copies	____ copies at $6.25 each

Name _____

Job Title _____

Organization _____

Address _____

City, State _____ Zip Code _____

Country _____ Phone _____ Fax _____

Email _____

Purchase order number (if applicable) _____

*Applicable sales tax, shipping, and handling charges
will be added. Prices subject to change.
Orders less than $250 require prepayment.
Standard shipping is FedEx 3-Day unless otherwise specified.*

☐ Check Enclosed   ☐ Please Invoice

☐ **VISA**   ☐ **MasterCard**   ☐ **AMERICAN EXPRESS**

Name on Card _____

Card Number _____ Expiration Date _____

Signature _____ Date _____

TO ORDER
By phone: 800-992-5922
Online: www.pritchettnet.com
Call for our mailing address or fax number.

P R I T C H E T T
Dallas, Texas